Peak District Poetry

Peter J. Marsden-Fereday

Peak District Poetry
Peter J. Marsden-Fereday
The Hallamshire Press 1996

Published by The Hallamshire Press
The Hallamshire Press is an Imprint of
Interleaf Productions Limited
Broom Hall
8–10 Broomhall Road
Sheffield S10 2DR
UK

Typeset by Interleaf Productions Limited
Printed by Saik Wah Press Pte. Ltd, Singapore

British Library Cataloguing in Publication Data
A catalogue record for this book is available from the British Library

ISBN 1-874718-09-1

Contents

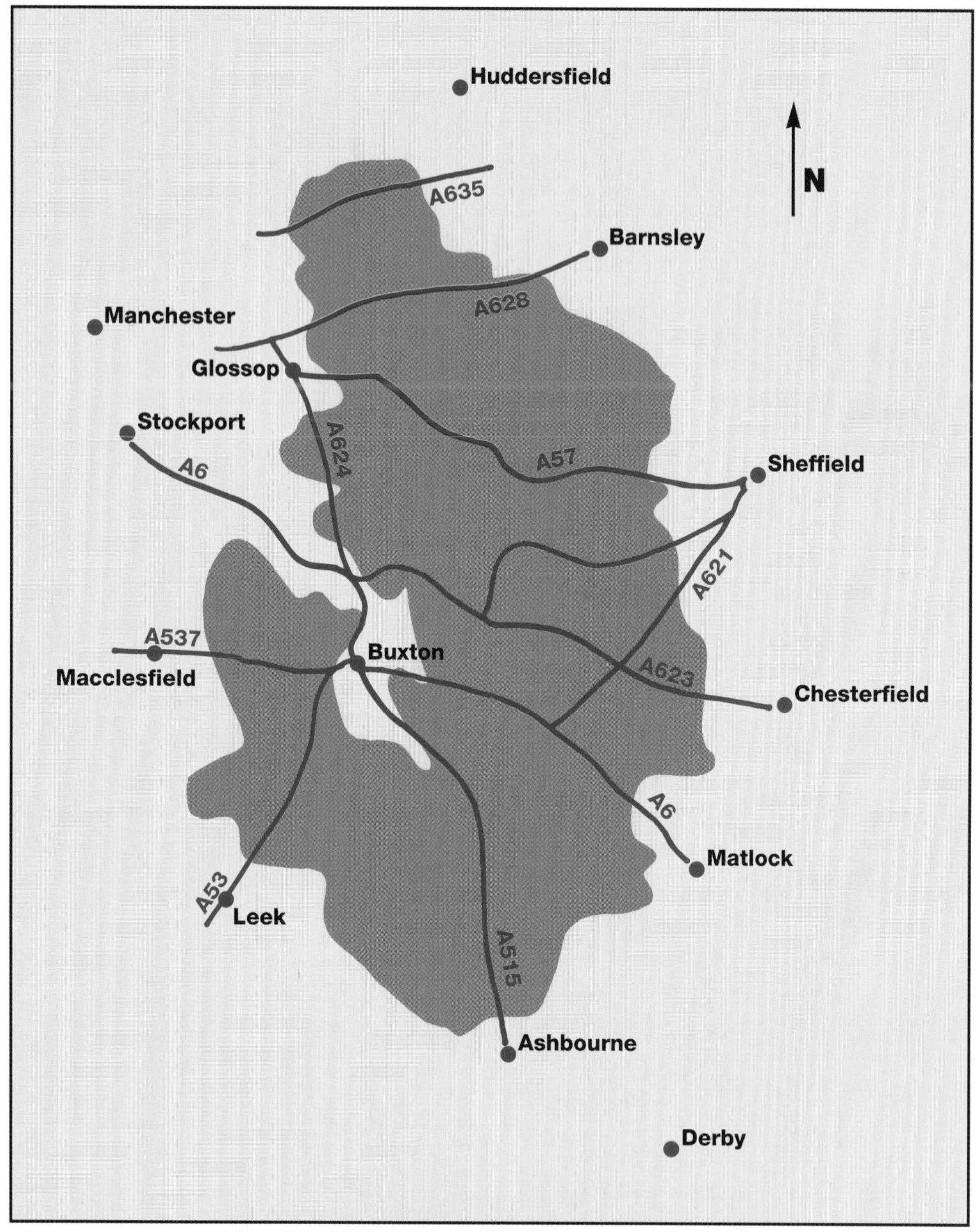

Peak District National Park

The Countryman

Enter into my open house
Amid the white and purple heather,
Beneath the sky which opens wide
Above my face of leather.
No walls no doors
Nor concrete floors,
No chairs, nor e'en a bed;
For 'tis my home
Where I belong
And where I lay my head.

Looking down from Curbar Edge one winter's evening, the village takes on a ghostly appearance as the Derwent Valley is flooded in a sea of cloud.

The Quiet Woman

She would nag him in the morning
She would nag him in the night;
She nagged him when he went to bed
Until the broad daylight.

She nagged him when he served the ale,
She nagged beyond repair;
She even nagged him when they kissed
And when he wasn't there.

'Enough, enough,' he cried one day
Unto his nagging bride;
'No quiet woman lies within
But one will hang outside.'

A headless woman now displays
The swinging tavern sign:
A warning to all nagging wives
Who to their spouses whine.

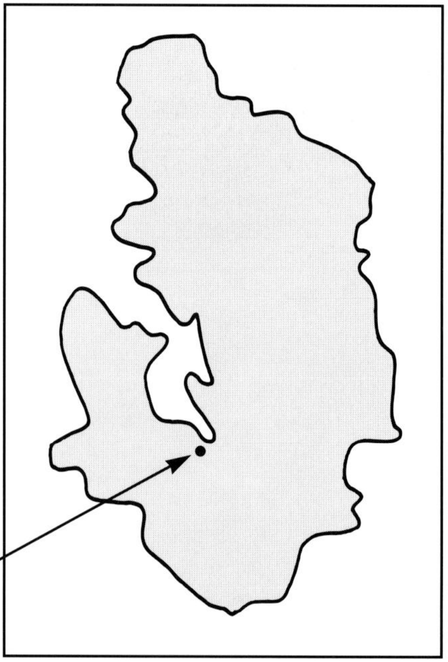

The Quiet Woman Inn, Earl Sterndale

This pleasant pub is found two miles north of Longnor.

150

Kinder Mass Trespass (1932)

Where now upon this common ground,
Which locals claim their outward bound;
No rights of way had long deterred
Encroachment of the human herd.

To view the hills from distant plains,
In wild abandon those terrains;
Their secrets ever to withhold
From ramblers who would tread so bold.

By bus and tram the masses came,
From towns and cities rolled the train;
To force the law upon the land
Whereon they stood to make their stand.

Young Benny Rothman led the men
Through thicket dense and open glen;
To reach the climb on Kinder Scout
With joyous song and fervent shout.

From both sides of the Pennine Way
Did Yorks and Lancs unite this day;
As Staffordshires from Peakland now
Met Derby men on Kinder's brow.

All cheering each, the other side
With passion deep and burning pride;
In vain the keepers of these lands
Retreated with their hired hands.

The freedom now which we enjoy,
We owe to every man and boy,
Who on that day, in thirty-two,
Bequeathed this trust that we may view.

Kinder Scout

A wide plateau of wild and isolated moorland.

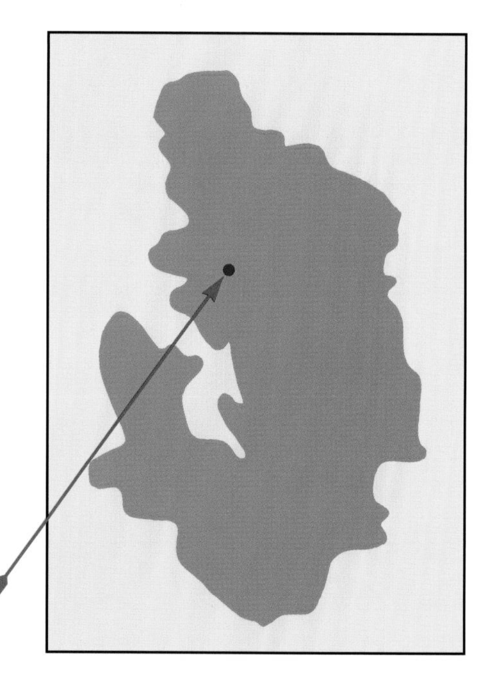

Flagg Races

Deerstalker hats
And wellies green,
Barber coats
And Harris tweed;
Walking sticks
And briar pipes,
The make-up
Of the country types.
Round and round
The old nags race,
The wind and rain
Hard in their face;
Laughter course,
Sorrows drowned,
All upon this
Sodden ground.
Bank holidays
And point-to-point,
Arthritis
And a twisted joint;
A good day out
By all was had,
When they raced
At lonely Flagg.

Flagg Races

Held every Easter Tuesday. The event is well signed from the A515.

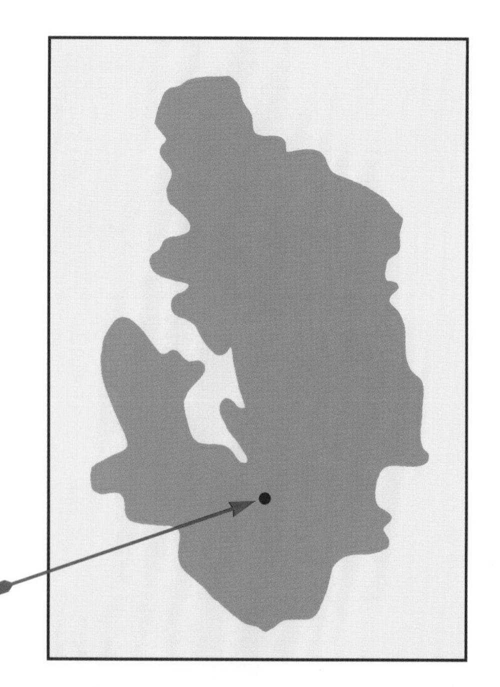

The Lead-Miners

Atop the hills where springs the rills,
The hardened miner climbs;
No time to pause
About his cause
Whilst trudging to the mines.

Down gaping holes, like human moles
To mother earth's bowels;
To work her veins
For meagre gains
With shovels, picks and trowels.

Each day is night and night is day,
The lanterned helmet shines;
With clothes of grey
All watered tight,
They work the leaded mines.

Slithering to, slithering fro,
Knowing not where they go;
In warrened halls
Of floods and falls
To work these slimy walls.

Emerging when their task is done,
Now gone the light of day;
Then homeward bound
To wife and hound
With pittance for their pay.

He mines the lead until he's dead,
The widow hides her grief;
In father's steps
Sons take the depths
In toil for their reliefs.

So it went, 'til the lead was spent
No more the mine to spoil;
The landlord boss
Wept not his loss
Which was the miner's toil.

The Lead-Miners Law
(from Manilove's poem)

On the third offence, for the stealing of lead: 'Shall have a knife stuck through his hand to the haft—or loose himself by cutting loose his hand; and shall forswear the franchise of the mine, and always lose his freedom from that time.'

Magpie Mine

Near Sheldon, three miles west of Bakewell. The site is open to the public and at weekends members of the Peak District Mines' Historical Society will often show visitors around the site.

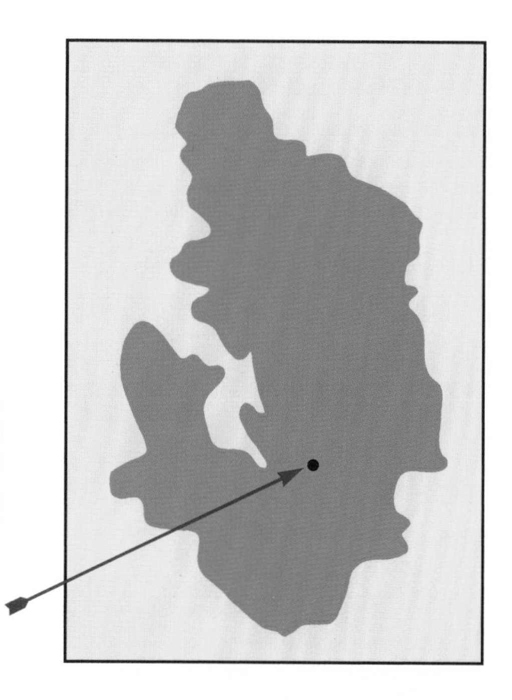

The Ballad of Molly Bray (The Ashford Dwarf: 1722–1811)

Oh dear sweet little Molly Bray,
Of fortunes she had none;
She sat beside the dusty road
In hope that hearts be won.

Her legs tucked underneath her cloak,
A teardrop in her eye;
The coaching party's pity took
To her just three feet high.

When day was done, she walked the road,
With pipe and knobbly stick;
Home to her cottage thatched and low,
Lit by a candle wick.

Eccentric though she might have been,
To her wrongs made no right;
But though her presence fixed the day,
Was never seen at night.

A neighbour said she was a witch,
Her neighbour did she catch;
A-flirting with old soldier John
Where then a plot she hatched.

Insisting that they both be wed,
Respected and revered;
She married them on broomstick high
As spells she knew they feared.

Throughout the Peak they came to know
Of dear sweet Molly Bray;
Who outlived all within those parts
Until she passed away.

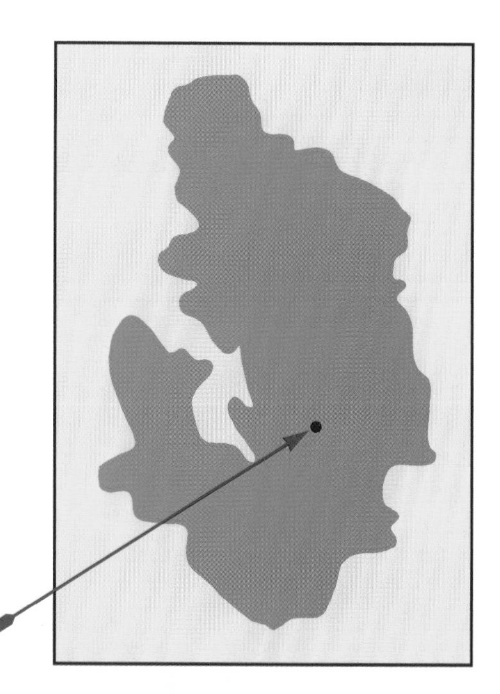

Ashford in the Water

The beautiful Sheepwash Bridge over the River Wye.

The Eyam Plague (1665–1666)

From London came the dreaded plague
To Eyam's fair village to invade;
Bound tight in dampened sewing cloth
To Mr Vickers' tailor's shop.

When opened up and aired to dry,
The germs ensnared now free did fly;
To swiftly spread the village o'er
All those therein, and many more.

During this time now such was Eyam,
A village placed in quarantine;
The Rector Stanley prayed within
Whilst Mompesson preached from the rim.

From vantage point that all could see,
He bent his back then bent his knee;
In prayer he bade them keep good faith
And in their weakness thanks they gave.

Mompesson then their needs did swell,
With food and clothing by the well;
In vinegar their coins they laid,
All due respect, their payment made.

In deep remorse Mompesson turned,
His wife now plagued, for whom he yearned;
Descending from his hillside flock,
Where o'er the dale they stood en bloc.

Seventeen score and ten poor souls
Which eighty-three survived their toils;
Helped by William Mompesson,
His faith, his hope and his sermon.

The Riley graves of Hancocks bold,
The cottages so plagued of old,
Mompesson's Well for all to see,
Remain in lasting memory.

Fair Eyam, thy sunbeams oft will play,
The birds shall sing both night and day;
And those who neither see nor hear
Shall sense the freedom of thy fear.

Plague Cottage at Eyam

Here the outbreak of the plague claimed its first victim in 1665. A stroll through this interesting old village will reveal plaques on many cottages commemorating those who died.

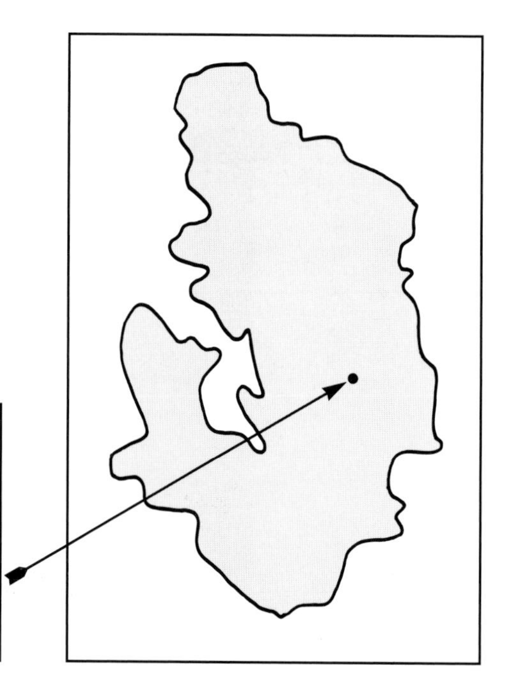

Tip (1954)

Such a hardy yet pleasant chore
When walking over Howden Moor;
But late December and New Year,
Leaves little for the Christmas cheer.

Distant clouds and a clear blue sky,
An urge to walk the hills on high;
Like Joseph Tagg and faithful Tip
When chancing on a Peakland trip.

As happens in the wild High Peak,
The unseen mists will promptly sweep;
Shrouding the hills with jealous guard,
Their trespass now held in regard.

Master and dog for fifteen weeks
Were never to descend those peaks,
'Til better climes found both ahead,
Though Tip survived, poor Tagg was dead.

Man's best friend had prevailed with pride,
Never to leave her master's side;
With a stone the High Peak honours,
Close by, the Dambuster Bombers.

Derwent

Looking across Ladybower reservoir to Derwent Edge.
Tip's memorial is to be found alongside the Upper Derwent Valley Road by Derwent Dam.

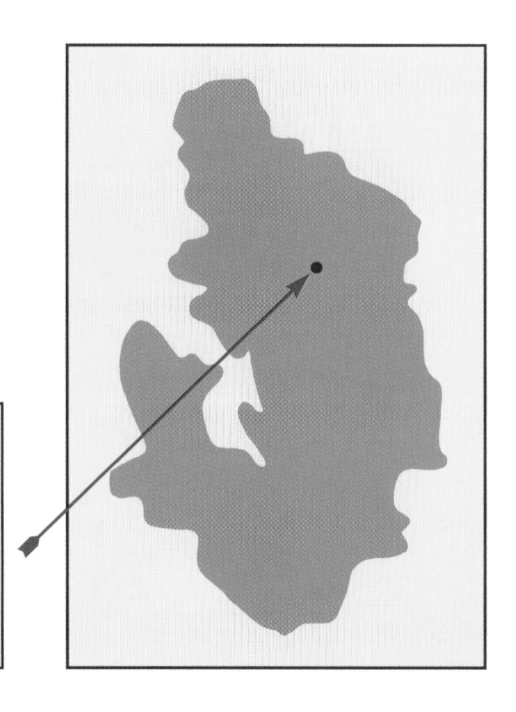

Daft Sammy (Samuel Eyre of Castleton: 1806–1868)

'Look yon', there runs Daft Sammy,'
The locals would all cry;
As Sammy o'er the hills would run
To a stagecoach passing by.

'Must be visitors in Castleton,'
They would gently muse;
For Sammy was of his village proud
To show off all its views.

Although by day the lead-mines called
To gain his weekly toil;
The moment Sammy's day was done
He'd seek out one and all.

A copper here, a copper there,
For e'er his needs to gain;
From strangers who would pay him heed,
When to his village came.

He'd tell them tales of the caverns,
Blue John and Mam Tor;
Peveril's Keep, the Winnats Pass
And many many more.

The ladies o'er the rills he'd help
Then gently set them down;
But if their escorts made no gift
He would follow them around.

Sammy soon was to become
The unofficial guide;
He put away his miner's tools
Until the day he died.

Not so daft then was our Sammy,
'Clever' would be more apt;
As was his lovely Castleton
So beautifully mapped.

Castleton

Visitors still flock to Castleton, especially in December when the village is decorated with illuminated Christmas trees.

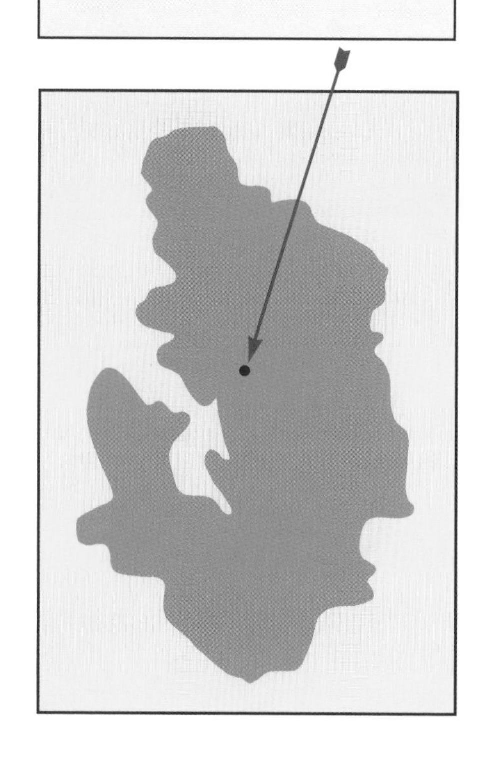

PEVERIL OUTDOOR
OUTDOOR CLOTHING CAMPING EQUIPMENT
SUZUKI
M644 VAK
G574 OWF

Peveril Castle

Rest now ye Norman on thy steed,
Yon castle then to thee take heed,
For once a Saxon held this place
Until the Conqueror did deface.
Our heritage is not of thine
Nor will it ever be but mine,
For we are English, Welsh and Picts,
The Celts of Ireland make us Brits.
Peveril Castle stands four-square
To every tempest everywhere;
Up high in solemn prominence
And based on Saxon eminence.
Above the steep Peak Cavern's mouth
With moorland heathers to the south;
Cave Dale's gully drops to the west
Where to the east Hope Valley's blessed.
'Sacrilege' I say unto thee,
To use this as a venery.
What softness ails the Norman head?
For better be a Saxon dead.

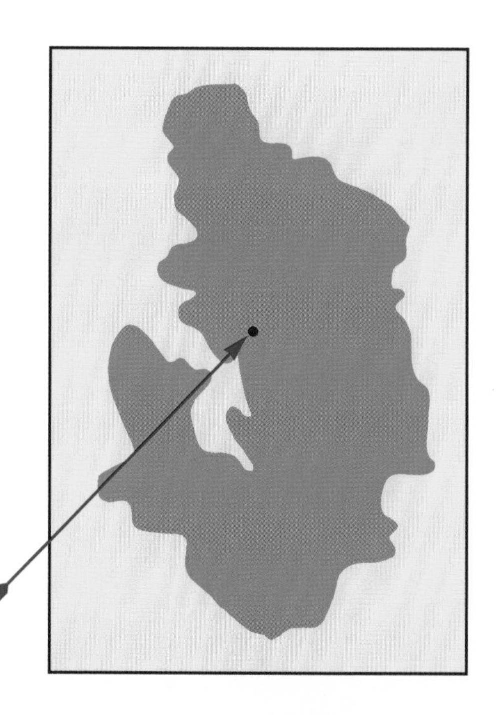

Peveril Castle

A spectacular view of Peveril Castle with Mam Tor in the background. The castle is open daily and can be visited by a short but steep track from Castleton village.

Doctor's Gate

Since Merlin ruled this magic land,
The Devil rose to take his stand;
But reckoned not with this dale,
For there was one who would him fail.

Known locally as 'Doctor Faust',
He swore the Devil he could oust;
Pledging his soul, his challenge met,
The Devil came for him to net.

They raced along the Roman road,
Where from Melandra legions strode;
An easy lead the Devil took,
'Til halted by a flowing brook.

The Doctor knowing all full well
His soul was not to go to hell;
The water being the Devil's loss
For which a spectre cannot cross.

Rejoicing at the Doctor's win,
This dale its magic kept within;
Though yet the Devil lies in wait,
He'll never bridge the 'Doctor's Gate'.

Doctor's Gate

A Roman trans-Pennine road, forerunner of the A57 and linking Glossop with Hope. Doctor's Gate can be seen near the summit of Snake Pass.

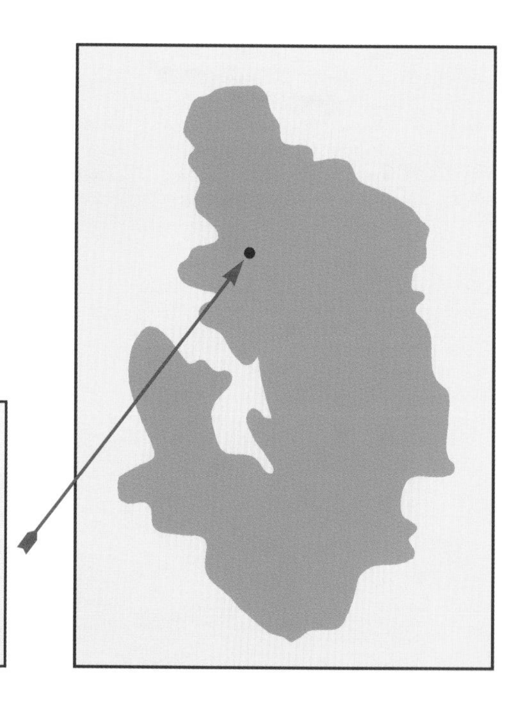

Samuel Slack (Tideswell Singer: 1737–1822)

He sang the songs of righteous men,
With hearty gusto and amen;
His basso voice fair shook the Peak,
An audience they came to seek.

He soon was known throughout the land,
Portraying all extremely grand;
The Duchess would no credit ask,
For lessons paid by her to task.

But Samuel Slack had appetite,
For brewer's pot and smoking pipe;
Indulging far beyond excess,
His public never would him guess.

Not for him the courteous courts,
The Peak being ever in his thoughts;
But more of wild abandon gay,
To fight with bulls in fields of hay.

Tideswell

The grave of Samuel Slack, a famous nineteenth century singer, can be found in the churchyard of St John the Baptist, Tideswell, known locally as the *Cathedral of The Peak*.

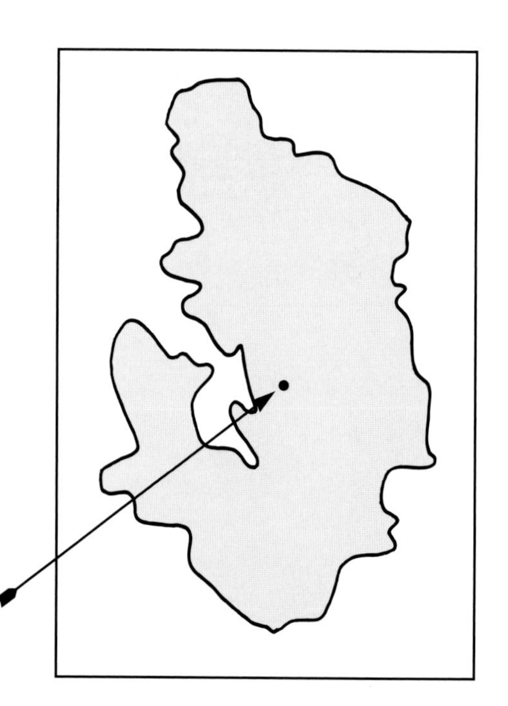

Buxton Road, Tideswell.
79665. JV

Mary Queen of Scots (Journey to Sheffield Castle: 1570)

Against the chill November morn,
When Kings and Queens lay snug and warm;
In Chatsworth's grand and courtly yard,
Cloaked and hooded was Shrewsbury's ward.

No common party tripped this day,
Ascending hills and moorland way;
But escorts of the captive Queen,
Her dangers held in high esteem.

On single tracks the ghostly train
Rode Froggatt Edge and wild terrain;
The purple heather waved no more,
Now bleak and brown the brackened floor.

With each peak, the elements grew,
Where in the wind the discourse blew;
Lost was Mary's call for repose,
Rejection of her pains and woes.

At last the downward trek began,
The seven hills of Sheffield scanned;
The castled walls, the drawbridge down,
Awaited now, the Scottish crown.

With head held high in stately pose,
Bedraggled, wet and torn her clothes;
She proudly through the portals rode,
In disregard to all abroad.

Such ills to bear, such baneful keeps,
Where all alone she gently weeps;
With hopes of what then might have been;
The English throne for Scotland's Queen.

Froggatt Edge

Mary's route between Chatsworth and Sheffield would involve crossing this high gritstone edge.

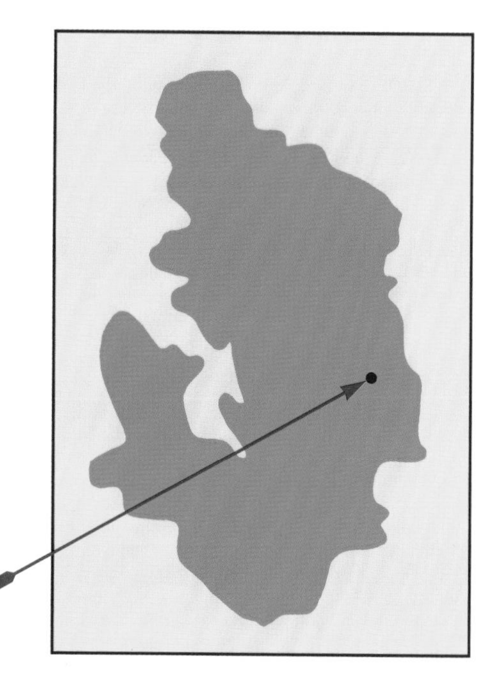

Cockeye's Ghost

Tellers of tales, singers of songs,
With raucous laughter all night long;
No fear have they who mine the lead,
Of lively souls or ghouls long dead.

The tale of which was told this night,
Was of a ghostly lady sprite,
Who haunted Cockeye's homeward path
In wait for those who chose to laugh.

Tom 'Cockeye' Loxley long did boast
Of Middleton Dale's lady ghost;
How he would, when the time arose,
Never flinch, but pinch her nose.

When mine host of the old Ball Inn,
At midnight then called time within;
Cockeye's courage began to fail,
His needs to soak his throat with ale.

More ale was served and flowing free,
When mine host closed the inn at three;
The revellers bade the night farewell
As to the morn their form then fell.

Fuddled with drink and tales of woe,
Cockeye adjudged which way to go;
By silent road and trickling rill,
He staggered home alone at will.

Cottages loomed aside the road,
The last one being the ghost's abode;
In wild amazement Cockeye froze,
As spectral guise with cries arose.

In fright he fell upon his face,
The spectre then did him embrace;
Her shadow over him did leer,
His drunken form now torn with fear.

Back down the dale she sped him fast,
Her icy hands his ankles clasped;
The chill began to freeze his heart,
His brain the cold did fold life's part.

With the light the following morn,
Mine host found Cockeye's drunken form;
Outside the inn, his ankles deep,
Half in the stream, his dream complete.

Middleton Dale

Lovers' Leap, Stoney Middleton and the Mill Stream.

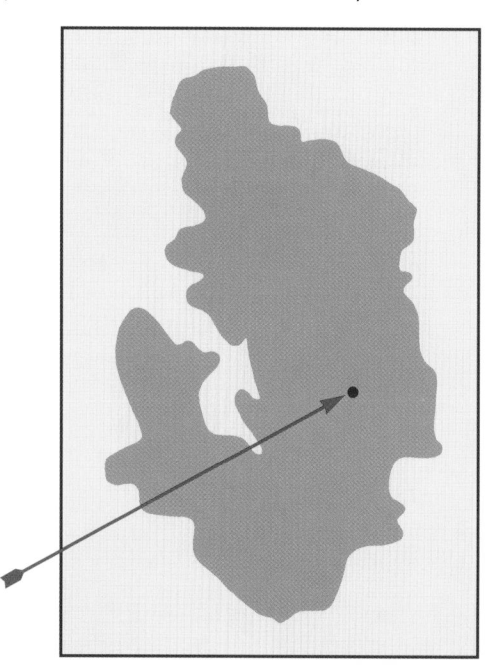

CAFE

Totley Tunnel

White rabbits on the heath abound,
Often as not, on Bleaklow found;
One did appear on Totley Moor,
To build a warren 'neath the floor.

It burrowed deep beneath these wastes,
To disappear with lightning haste;
For all was left, this gaping hole,
No sign of life by which it stole.

From Sheffield to the Peakland Park,
Throughout this tunnel dank and dark;
It sped along the sleepers' tracks,
Through sunlit rays from chimney stacks.

No stopping for a breathing space,
As on and on the rabbit raced;
As if by which to make up time,
For wasting life on things sublime.

Deceiving is the distant light,
When first the exit is in sight;
But, oh what joys now close at hand,
When Grindleford springs wonderland.

Totley Tunnel

A 'single-wheeler' rushes out of the three and a half mile long Totley Tunnel, heading an express train from Manchester to Sheffield. The Midland Railway Company opened the Hope Valley Line in 1894.

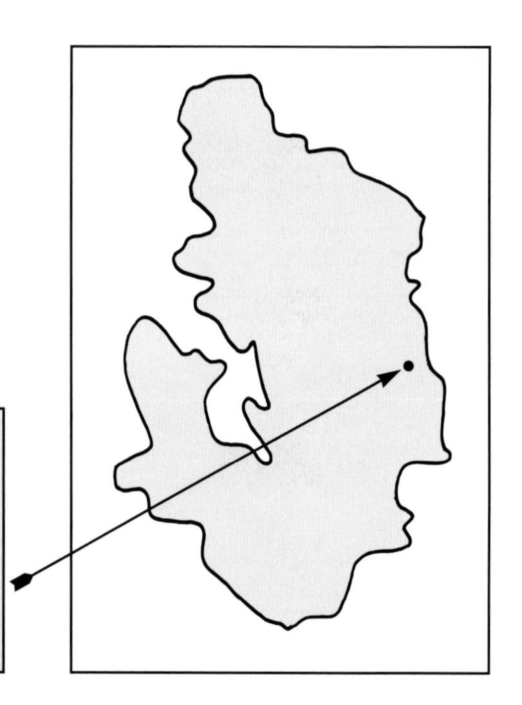

TOTLEY TUNNEL
TOTLEY
TUNNEL
6230 YARDS.
M R
TOTLEY TUNNEL, MIDLAND RAILWAY.

The Wizard and the Witch

From Monsal Head, view Monsal Dale,
This magic land of fairy tale;
Where hobs and sprites,
Witches and fays,
All dance beneath the sunlit rays.

Within this dale, a wizard lurked,
Where once upon his spells he worked;
Neddy Higgins,
And Betty too,
His daughter, who on broomsticks flew.

Although with caution both were sought,
Their charms a reputation brought;
With fortunes told
And spells curtailed,
Problems they solved where others failed.

Within the recess of a rock
They prophesied unto the flock;
A stolen sheep,
A thorny plight,
Their foretelling to all was right.

So come and dance this merry vale,
With fairies all in Monsal Dale;
Beneath the bridge,
Aside the stream,
On still these pleasant pastures green.

Monsal Dale

Monsal Dale Viaduct, until the coming of Dr Beeching in the 1960s, formed part of the Midland Railway's main route from London, St Pancras, to Manchester. It now forms part of the Monsal Trail footpath.

Left: Upperdale Bridge.

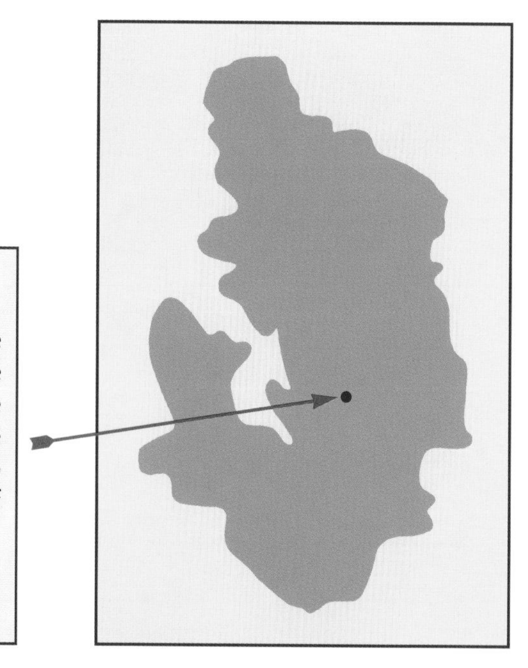

Lost Lad

This foreboding land of marsh and heather,
Strange formations and varying weather;
No place, then, here for the tentative soul,
But strictly compassed for a hardy toil.
Sturdy was the young adventuresome lad,
By aiding the hunt, experience had;
Though a sapling of a mere thirteen years
He knew no bounds; nor had no fears.
So upon the call of quadrupeds lost
Did he race the storm, regardless the cost;
Through the elements, towards Derwent Edge,
Shouting and whistling, his life did he pledge.
For how long he searched, no one seems to know,
As he hid in the rocks, out of the snow.
For a whole three months they searched for the lad,
On the moor where snow was heavily clad;
It was then a shepherd was heard to cry,
Whereupon all the rest came to espy;
Never before was there a sight so sad,
As beside his body he scratched 'Lost Lad'.

The Shepherd's Tribute

In respect of 'Lost Lad', upon where he was found,
Stands a mammoth-size cairn, rising up from the ground.
A shepherd on passing will place there by hand
A stone on the cairn, whene'er walking this land.

Derwent Edge

Lost Lad Cairn is on the flank of Derwent Edge, seen here across Derwent Reservoir in the Upper Derwent Valley.

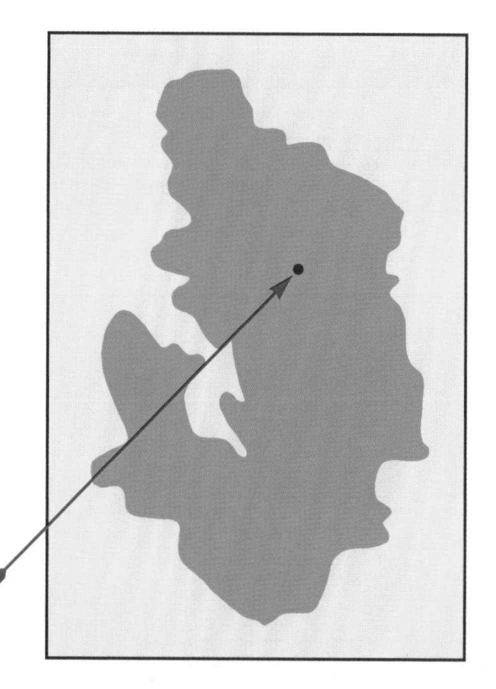

The Unhappy Prince

'Unhappy Royal Prince, mourn not that fate which is not thine.'

North of Bakewell by Four Lane Ends,
Where at the cross do spectres tend;
On grassy bank, no joys to task,
Prince Arthur dared for favours ask.

With head held tight between his knees,
The spirits to him aimed to please;
He wished his soul for better life,
That he might have a darling wife.

A vision then came over him,
To suit his needs and every whim;
Though wed, he'd be in ecstasy,
Four months would 'lapse, then misery.

His death the vision ill was met,
His wishes granted, paid the debt;
His brother Henry took his throne
By which himself six wives did own.

Hassop

Three miles north of Bakewell. This tiny village is dominated by a massive and incongruous Roman Catholic church, built in classical style.

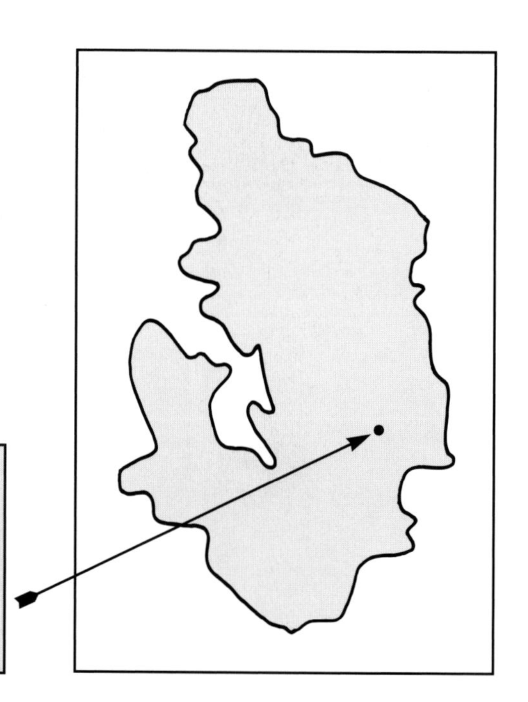

Hassop Village, Derbyshi

Mam Tor

Weathered are these shivering steeps,
Where hides the sun when peaceful sleeps;
Aloft the falls with ramparts round,
This iron-age fort on tribal ground.

Mam Tor, or 'mother hill' they say,
Stands now in beauteous decay;
Such is this awesome view to gaze,
From Castleton of ancient days.

Parental to her plain surrounds,
In jealous guard to outward bounds;
If ever foe would here then map,
As in her basin would be trapped.

This massive fortress to conclude,
Hope Valley and Carl Wark's prelude,
Did compliment each other's frame,
When torches lit their beacons' flame.

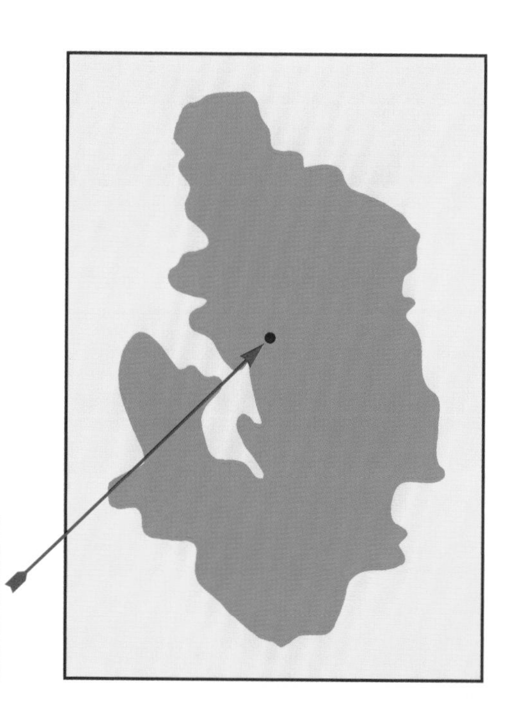

Mam Tor

A view of the 'Shivering Mountain' from Peveril Castle.

The Bakewell Witches (1608)

First Story

Mrs Stafford was a Milliner
In dear old Bakewell town,
Living with her sister
To sew both hat and gown.

One night there did a Scotsman call
To rent an upstairs room,
Who heard them a chanting
And baying to the moon.

'Over thick, over thin,
Now, Devil,
To the cellar in lunnon.'

Through cracks in the flooring
He saw their nightly dress,
Clothed for a journeying
It was the Scotsman's guess.

Repeating the rhyme they chanted,
Going through the motions too;
But where 'Over' was said,
His chant was changed to 'Through'.

A gush of air then scooped him high
And whisked him right afar,
Whereupon he was set nigh,
Beside them in the cellar.

The two witches' carryings-on
Quickly came to light,
Both went for execution
Upon the Scotsman's plight.

Second Story

The Scotsman having stayed 'til light
With ne'er a penny piece,
When found he couldn't pay the night,
His clothes paid for the lease.

Out on the road to London town
He vowed to have his way,
That Mrs Stafford's hats and gowns
Would have them witches say.

There in a cellar did he wait,
Catching the watchman's eye,
Who marched him to the magistrate
To hear the plaintiff's cry.

Half-naked in the court of law
His story he did tell,
Of London's chimneys down below
When 'neath the witches' spell.

From Bakewell town they casted him
With ne'er a stitch to wear,
Clothes then unto him were given
As did his tale he swear.

A witch-hunt then was put in force
To check the Scotsman's tale;
Off up to Bakewell did they course
Upon the witches' trail.

When Mrs Stafford came to greet,
They looked beyond the door,
And there piled neatly in a heap
The Scotsman's clothes they saw.

The story proven by his clothes
Did surely seal their fate,
For witches did they love to hunt
Then hold a hanging fête.

Bakewell

The thirteenth century bridge over the River Wye.

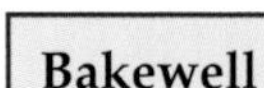

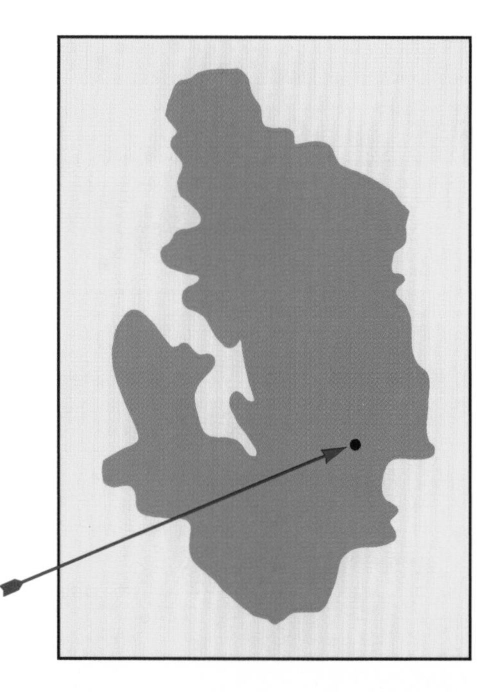

Little John of Hathersage

How long thou liest,
How deep thou sleepst,
Far from the greenwood glade,
Thy bow no longer by thy side,
Nor e'en the foeman's blade.

The peace for which
Thou sought with Hode,
Finds thee now in this abode;
Betwixt the yews
In St Michael's yard,
Fair Hathersage:
Care tend thy ward.

On eastern hill
Thy cottage still,
Though now in disrepair;
Couldst thou have been a nailer then,
When going to Nottingham Fair?

If death is sleep,
In sleep then dream,
Those feats of derring-do;
For thee John Little
A giant stood,
In history; through and through

Hathersage

The fourteenth century church of St Michael and All Angels, Hathersage.

The grave of Robin Hood's companion can be found in the churchyard.

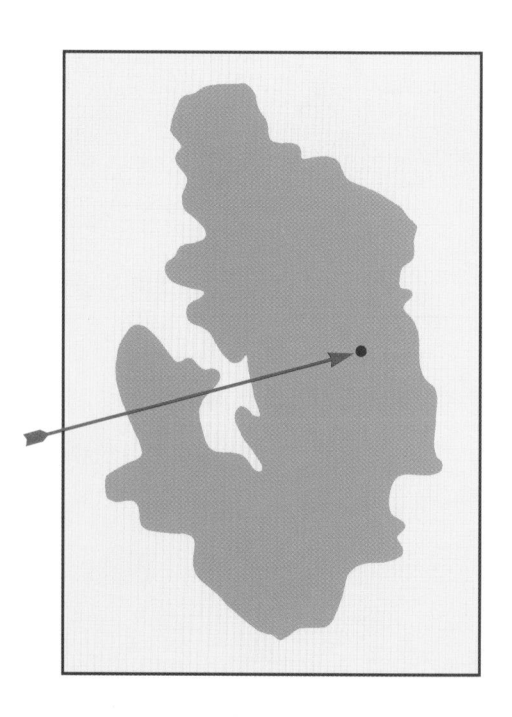

Eadwine and Pendor (The Battle of Lose Hill and Win Hill: 7th Century)

Two Saxon chiefs
To Peakrell came,
A Lady's honour
They sought to gain;
For Lilla they pledged
No turning back,
A battle loomed
The foe to sack.
Beacons were lit
Atop Lose Hill,
Blood-curdling cries
Let out at will.
Across the vale
Win Hill stood proud;
Penda's men rose
To Edwin's crowd.
They met the vale,
They met the hill,
They met the brow,
They met the kill;
A wasteless land
No ground to gain,
For all was up
Then down again.
With battle-axe,
Broadsword in hand,
They waged their war
O'er this brown land.
Each hill was took
Then took again,
'Midst the bodies
Of those were slain.
'Edwin', they cried
In victory,
'Penda', they claimed
For bravery.
Heathen brethren
Of both sides met,
Blood congealing
And blood yet let;
The camps were sacked
The beacons dowsed,
Dead were buried
The wounded roused.
No battle now
But dispute soared,
Of whom to wars
Would lead the horde.
One battle fought,
One battle less,
Two sides now joined
One to suppress.
No Christians here,
No Church nor priest,
But wolves and rites
In heathen feast;
For those survived,
The battle won,
Now took their fight
To peasantdom.
Pillage and rape
Of lowly farms,
Skirmishes where
Some took up arms;
No warring skills
The peasantry
In which to match
Such treachery.
The heathen horde
No mercy shown,
All in their path
Were rudely hewn.
In twilight now
The dark clouds rolled,
From Kinder Scout
The day to fold;
Wearied with sleep,
Warriors lay,
Scattered around
'Til break of day.
Shadowy ghosts
In combat still,
Their stifled cries
As each they kill.
The dying day
To night it yields,
Its fading light
Now dulls the shields;
Tomorrow's song
The bards will sing,
Of yesterday's
Wild 'Peakrell King'.

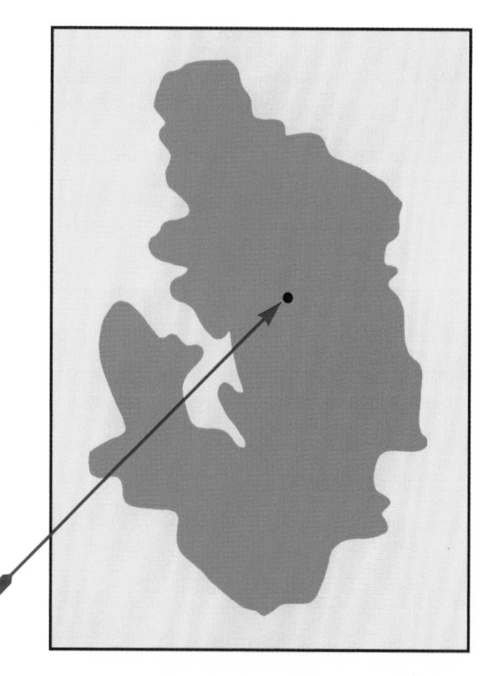

Lose Hill

Looking across to Lose Hill from the Edale Valley.

Murder at Winnats (1758)

Fresh as the wind which blows on high,
With cherried cheeks and looks so shy,
The smile of innocents did prevail
As they set foot in Middleton Dale.

From regions south the couple came,
'Pon hearing of Peak Forest's fame;
Eloping from their homely ties
To gain each other was their prize.

Grandly attired, their notice read
As from their steeds did lightly tread,
Upon his arm dear Clara walked
Whilst Allan did assuredly talk.

The landlord of the Royal Oak inn
Outstretched his arms and welcomed them,
Beds were made, a meal was served,
The horsed fed, their needs revered.

The morrow brought a joyous day,
Refreshed now from their nightly stay,
But Clara's thoughts were on her face
As Allan tried her grief to place.

Her dreams were not of wedded bliss,
More of life's dreaded deathly kiss,
For ills she dreamt during the night,
Of larceny and a fateful fight.

Good Allan put her mind at ease
As with her hand did gently squeeze,
Whereon they rode their steed upon
The winding road to Castleton.

Their berth so wide in which to take
Their kin if following, they hoped to shake,
But trace them if they ever should,
An easy task, the way they looked.

In Castleton they stayed awhile
But the inn they chose was coarse and vile,
Where uncouth men from Odin Mine
Held in contempt their clothes so fine.

The couple took their place inside
The miners to their saddlebags eyed,
A plot was hatched, the men did leave,
To further inns they made to weave.

After having fulfilled their needs,
The elopers then made for their steeds,
Peak Forest being their final call
By which to wed once and for all.

Up Winnats Pass they slowly walked,
Unbeknown they were being stalked,
The drunken miners laid in wait,
Then sprang them to secure their fate.

Poor Clara then began to scream
As she recalled her nightly dream,
Allan pleaded to no avail,
As he was dragged across the dale.

The plunder then began to start
Which broke the hapless Clara's heart;
Into a barn then they were thrown
Thus guarded by one man alone.

Allan, overpowering the man,
Then to the other four he ran,
He fought with all the skills he knew,
But with a pick then he was slew.

His bride-to-be was also slain,
Which left the killers in disdain;
The bodies now they had to hide
Which at the barn they left inside.

Three times did they to the barn return
In which the bodies to intern;
Three times, steeds and spectres appeared,
Two of each, both foaming and reared.

The bodies when at last laid low,
In Castleton two steeds did show,
Of thoroughbred and fully groomed
Village suspicions quickly loomed.

Did Eldon Hole the couple take,
Or did they stray o'er Dirtlow Rake?
Suspicions swiftly grew and grew
Of anyone with something new.

The miner's child, a pretty dress,
Trinkets bought by which to impress,
An extra night spent at the inn
With careless money, to a whim.

Unsolved, the mystery did remain
Until a miner's last refrain;
He told the story from his bed,
How he had killed, with four now dead.

An ironic twist in fate surrounds
Of all were present on those grounds,
One by one the murderers died
As if some unknown forces vied.
The first fell down a precipice,
Above the Winnats Pass.
The second from a falling rock,
Near to the lad and lass.
The third went absolutely mad,
And subsequently died.
The fourth did duly hang himself,
Committing suicide.
The fifth upon his story told,
When all was done and said;
Barely beat the scaffold,
When they pronounced him dead.

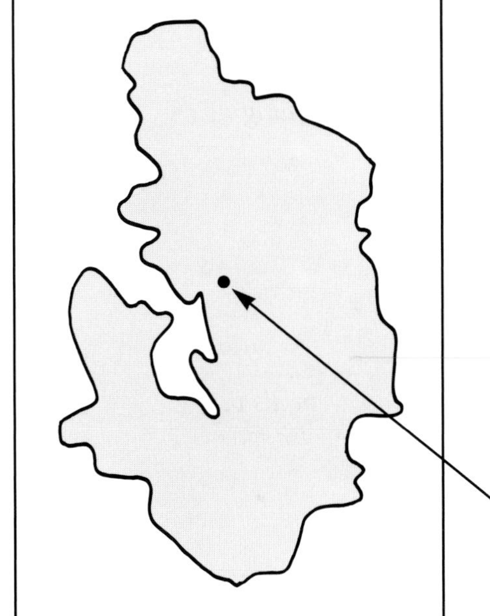

Winnats Pass

The Dambusters

The Derwent Dam in Derwent Dale
Its secret held the Ruhr's nail;
Barnes Wallis held a short intake
Until his brainchild skimmed the wake.

Now o'er the Derwent once again
In memory of this mighty plane;
To witness, yes, just one more time,
The squadron whom the dams did mine.

The engines droned and creaked with age,
Yet not in sight upon this stage;
The crowd in apprehension bide
Their timed nostalgic burning pride.

Then down the valley could be seen
The red and brown and mottled green;
Descending to the waters brink,
No bomb this time for which to sink.

Between the turrets did it pass
A loud and deafening metal mass;
Soaring high we did remember,
This the last, Lancaster Bomber.

Derwent Dam

The Lancaster flew over the turrets of Derwent Dam in May 1995 to commemorate the 50th anniversary of VE Day.

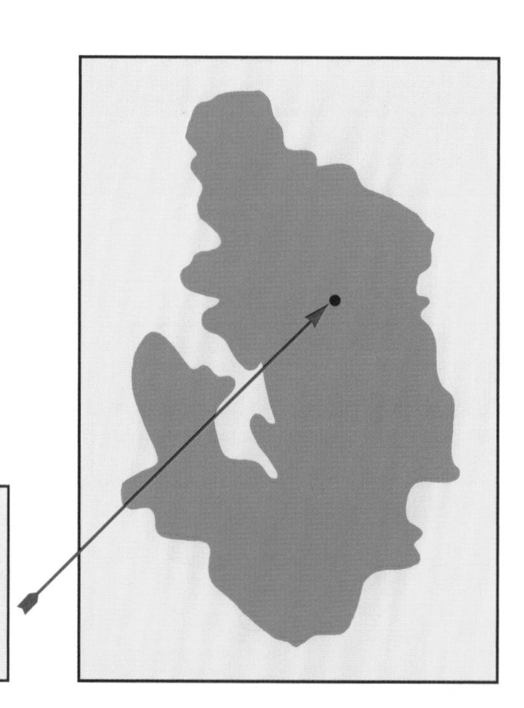

Graveyard of Planes (The High Peak)

Scattered debris lay all around,
Upon this high and misty ground;
Spitfire, Blenheim,
Lancasters too,
Are but to name a gallant few.

These hilltops claimed a full two-score
Of Britain's best and many more;
To navigate
Was no mean task,
When having Peakland to unmask.

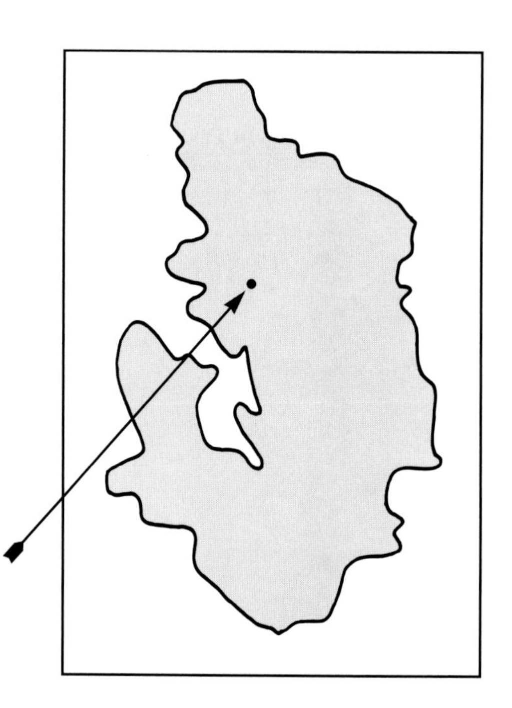

The High Peak

Blenheim IV, Z5870, 6 Anti-Aircraft Co-operation Unit, 12 Group, Flying from Digby to Ringway, crashed below Crowden Tower, Edale, July 3rd 1941.

D GB

Tissington Well

Never ending do they seem to weep,
These waters from the southern Peak;
Even in drought there are no fears,
With which to stem this flood of tears.

As if a miracle to behold,
These rushing waters pure and cold;
In thanks each year are truly blessed,
When each and every well is dressed.

Tissington

Well Dressing is a custom unique to Derbyshire. The wells are decorated with petals and leaves set in clay to form beautiful pictures. The dressing of the five Tissington wells is especially popular with visitors, for this is a most attractive village with its old hall and Norman church.

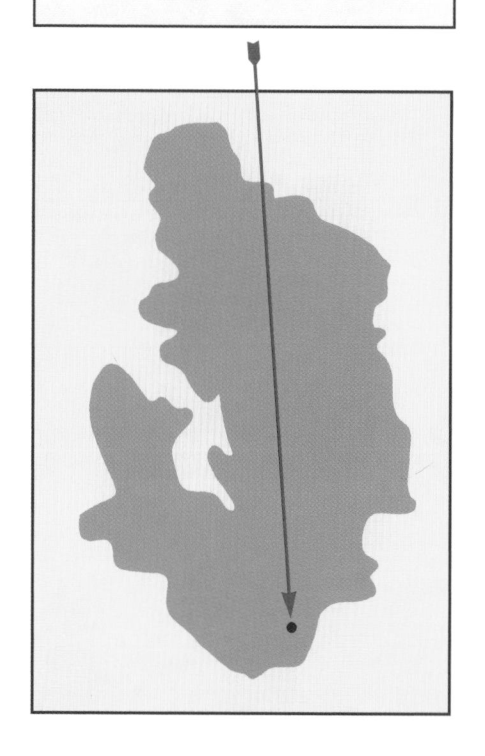

JESUS AND THE CHILDREN
19
TOWN WELL

Nine Ladies

Merrily danced the maidens fair,
High on Stanton Moor;
Dancing to the fiddler's tune
Upon this heathen floor.

Their dancing through the night did pass,
Until the day did dawn;
When all to stone were quickly turned
For shaming Sabbath's morn.

Now motionless nine ladies rest,
No longer holding hands;
The fiddler now a kingly stone,
With statues to command.

Stanton Moor

It is worth the walk up onto the heather-covered ridge, not only to find the stone circle, but for the splendid views across the Derwent Valley to Darley Dale and Riber Castle.

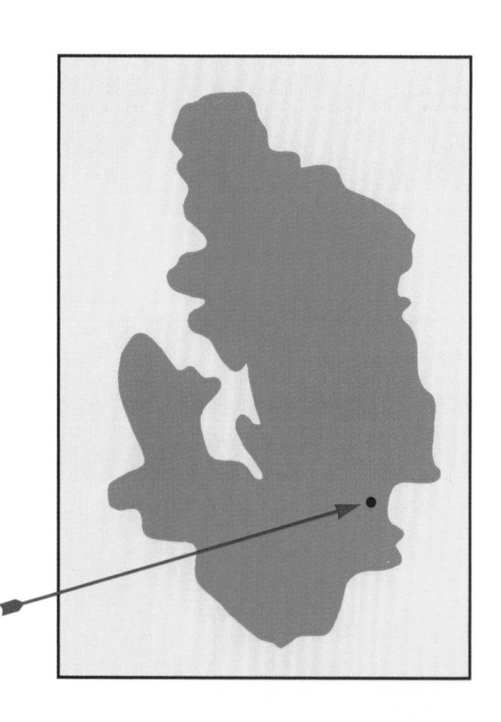

The Barlow Hunt

Happy are the hunter's hounds,
Merry the mounted men;
Ready to ride the rough terrain
Without, withal and when.

The fox forever furtive waits
The happy hunting horn;
Eerily echoing endlessly
To cheer the chase, the morn.

Tally-ho's: to horse, to horse,
The calls cry out to court;
When gone to ground the gallant guile
The pack repair to port.

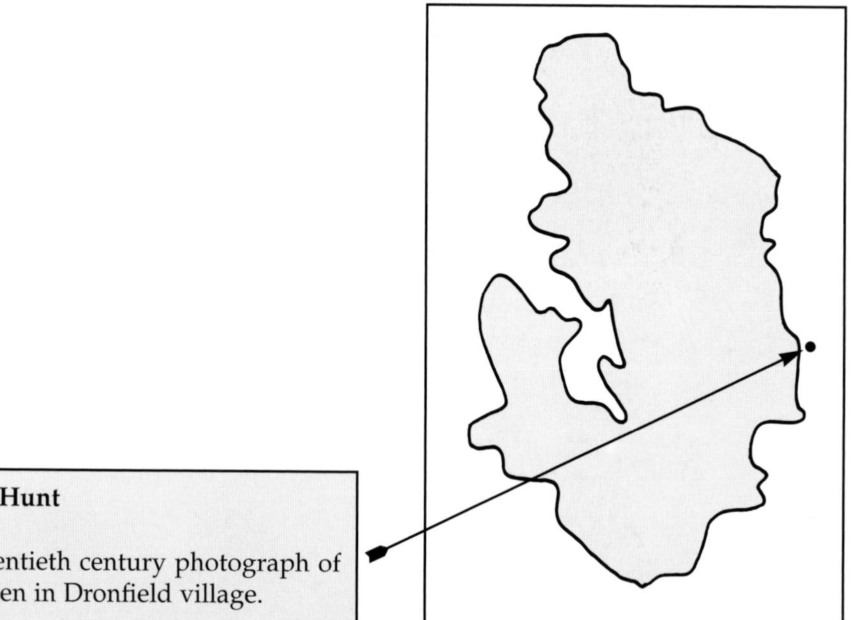

The Barlow Hunt

An early twentieth century photograph of the Hunt taken in Dronfield village.

The Bodysnatchers of Hope Valley

Though barely cold and in the grave,
With Christian rites the soul to save;
When laid to rest
Life's troubles eased,
The resurrectors stirred the peace.

The resurrection carts abound,
Throughout the night without a sound;
Conveying up
To Froggatt Edge,
Where at the Chequers deals are pledged.

Outside the inn the bodies rest,
Disguised withal to look their best;
Aloft a coach,
Aside a gate,
No ale for those who met their fate.

When all the dealing then is done,
To Padley Woods the web is spun;
The bodies there
To decompose,
With ants to aid the medics' cause.

The Chequers Inn

The Inn nestles beneath the imposing grit-stone escarpment of Froggatt Edge beside the B6054.

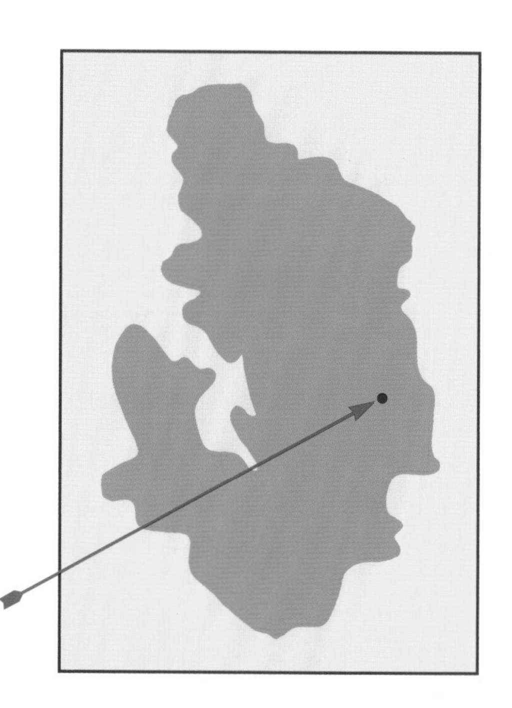

WARDS
Chequers
Inn

Bakewell Market

Hasten ye then to Bakewell town
On an early Monday morn,
Tek tea or coffee
Wi' Bakewell pud
Or if you please—
A scone.
Then it's off ta market wi' cattle rare
Where there's an auction ring,
The caller calls so very fast
Tha can almost hear him sing.
In pens laid out the cattle wait
Wi' labelled pasted backs,
Their unkempt skins
Not tarted up.
Wi' bamboo, herdsman smacks:

Cows an' calves wi' baleful eyes,
Bulls and bullocks all shapes an' size,
Woolly sheep
An occasional goat,
An trout in't river, which teks no float.
Out of one pen
Inta t'other,
Awaiting auctioneer;
After that t' highest bidder
Then farmer's off to have a beer.
T'other market's fer their counterparts,
Those graceless human beings;
Herded together
'Twixt little stalls
Packed tight just like sardines.

But all in all,
Not a bad day out
For townie and farmer alike;
It all depends
Just wot tha wants
Or if tha't on a hike.

Bakewell

The auctioneer, hammer in hand, accepts a bid made by the farmer plunging his hand into the sheep's fleece at the cattle market.

Left: Tranquility amongst the spring flowers in the public gardens.

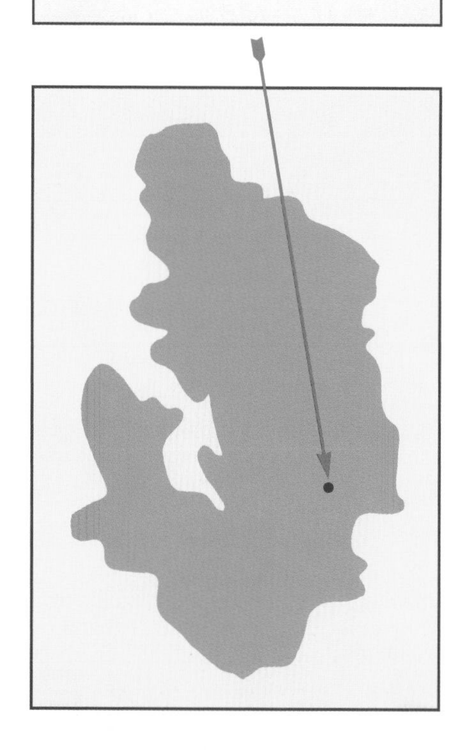

Bakewell Pudding

Misunderstanding of a person's needs,
Is sometimes greater than a thousand deeds;
Likened to the cook at the Rutland Arms,
Who chanced a recipe of secret charms.

The mistress Greaves ordered strawberry tart,
Egg into pastry with jam the top part;
But cook poured the mix on top of the jam,
Making a pudding instead of a flan.

Out of the oven and served to the guests,
Their cheery faces did 'seconds' request;
The cook when enquired, 'What can I say?'
Was told: 'Continue to make it that way.'

Bakewell

The Rutland Arms Hotel in the Square, looking towards the parish church of All Saints.
Behind the photographer is the 'Old Bakewell Pudding Shop' where this special delicacy can still be purchased.

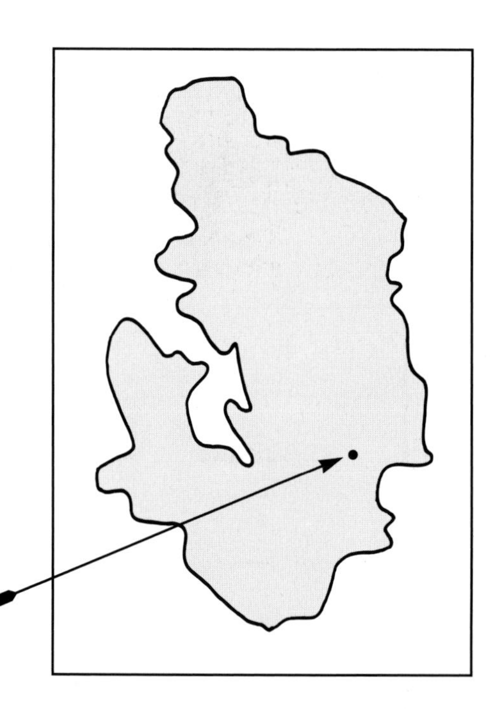

The Rutland Arms Hotel, Bakewell.

Robin Hood's Stoop

The arrowhead was shafted long,
The bow nigh tall as he;
Which coursed the flight
Both true and strong,
Across the wide Hope Valley.

From Offerton to Hathersage,
The distant arrow flew;
To land close by
John Little's grave,
Beneath St Michael's yew.

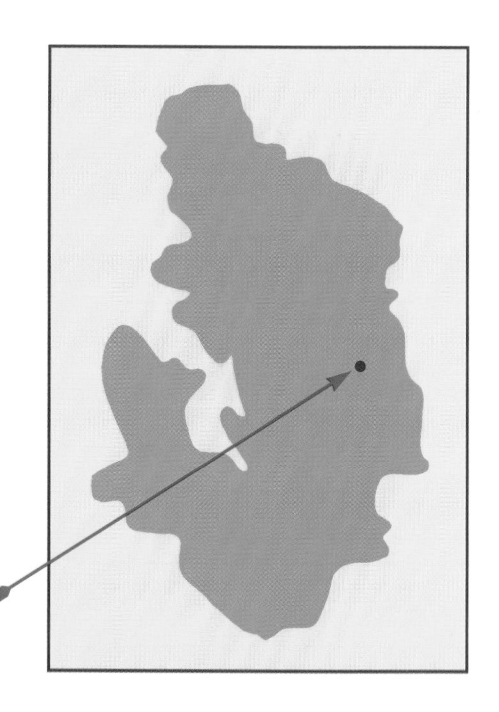

Offerton Moor

Robin Hood's Stoop lies on the eastern rim of Offerton Moor, seen here from the public footpath on the banks of the Derwent near Hathersage.

Lover's Leap

No truer love
In life can hold;
Than to die
When half grows cold.
Dear Hannah Baddaley
She gave her all,
To William Barnsley
Whose love did fall.
Heartbroken as
Poor Hannah was,
Her love she knew
To be so true,
Without repair
Nor to replace,
She leapt the leap
Down past its face.
Uprushing winds
Ballooned her skirts,
As gently down she fell;
To live again
Saved by the fates;
But ventured not
To love as well.

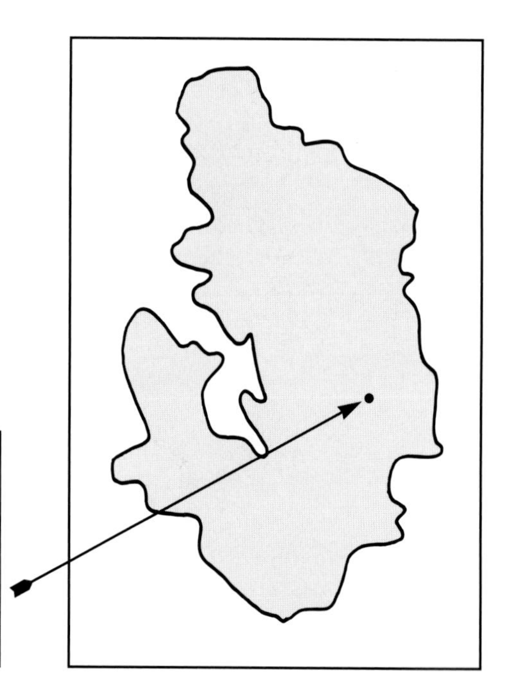

Stoney Middleton

The eighty-foot cliff at Stoney Middleton, from which Hannah leapt. The quiet lane in the picture is now the busy A623 road through Middleton Dale.

LOVERS LEAP
INN
Middleton Dale
At the Lover's Leap
M&S. 1726.

Queen Mary's Bower

What holds the secret of this bower?
What there was kept within?
Such lofty steps
For a restful hour,
To ease a sovereign's whim.

A folly, perhaps, built in renown,
Soon after Mary's fall;
Her coat of arms
Defying the crown,
May well had traitors call.

Chatsworth Park

Fallow deer in the Park.
The building of the great house was begun in 1552 by Bess of Hardwick. Her fourth husband, George Talbot—Earl of Shrewsbury, was custodian of the ill-fated Mary Queen of Scots, who was held prisoner at Chatsworth at various times between 1569 and 1584.

Left: Queen Mary's Bower.

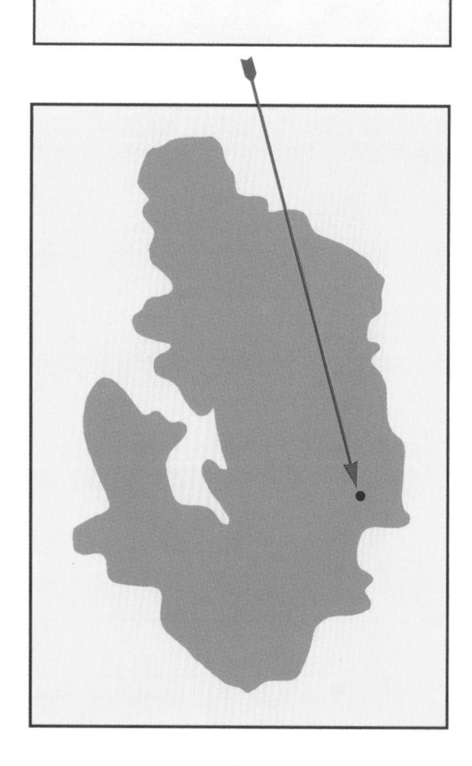

The Longdendale Lights

Searching, moving, fading lights,
Lights that light
The sky at night;
Bluish-white and shining bright
Yet when approached are out of sight.

Troglodytes, mischievous sprites,
Fairy lights
Do souls invite;
Dancing 'neath the starry night,
Reflections of a Roman site.

Meteorites, alien flights,
Flares of fright
From ramblers' plights;
What illuminates these heights
That bathes in floodlight Bleaklow's might?

Longdendale

Looming over the hamlet of Crowden in Longdendale are the long-derelict quarries of Hey Edge.

So desolate are these moors that the Pennine Way which once passed here has now been re-routed.

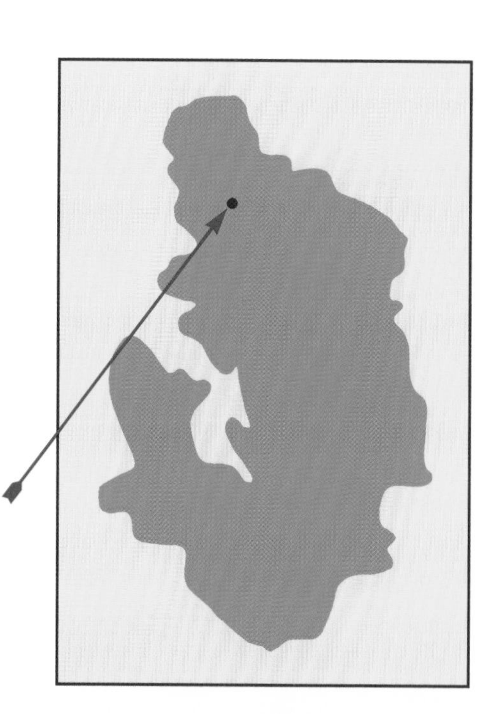

The Deep Dale Fairies

In Deep Dale on a Friday morn
'Tis full of sadness, full of scorn;
Take heed the warning
Wear not green,
Lest you offend the Fairy Queen.

This day of action and affairs
Is in extreme to mortal cares;
If discontented
And annoyed,
The fairies' wrath you can't avoid.

In darkened caves beneath the ground
Is where their sumptuous suites are found,
Banquets and dancing,
Fun and games,
Comely fays with enchanting names.

Such a call is hard to withstand
If offered by the fairies' hand,
But sit in quiet
And ne'er eat,
Nor take part in the fairies' fête.

For if upon their joys you share,
Yourself to them you will ensnare;
Observe them only
As when free;
Just waste and void is all you'll see.

Deep Dale

The visitor to this secret location must first brave the public footpath skirting the despoilation of Topley Pike Quarry. It is well signposted but requires agility and stout footwear.
Park in the public car park opposite the quarry entrance, where the A6 from Taddington towards Buxton drops steeply into the Wye Valley.

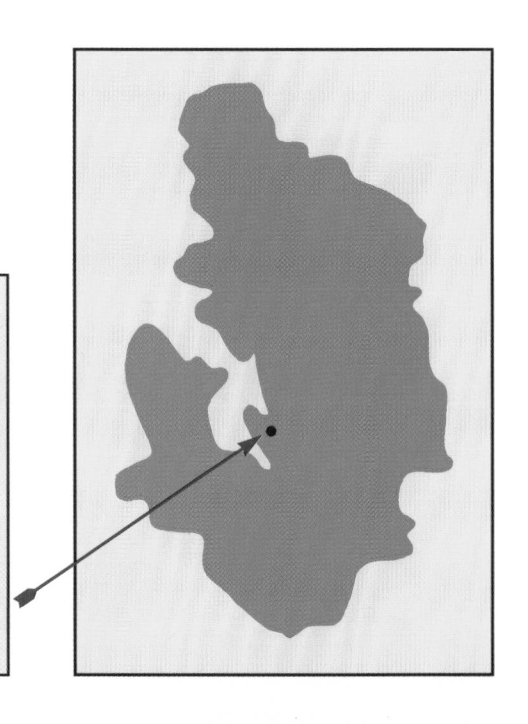

The Mermaid of the Peak

'She calls on you to greet her, combing her dripping crown
and if you go to meet her, she ups and drags you down.'

One minute past the midnight hour,
When Easter Sunday falls;
Edge close beside the Mermaid's Pool,
To hear the siren's calls.
Alone she swims this darkened pool,
Where cattle will not dine,
Its salty waters from the deep
Atlantic Ocean brine.

Kinder Scout

The Mermaid's Pool nestles below Kinder Downfall.

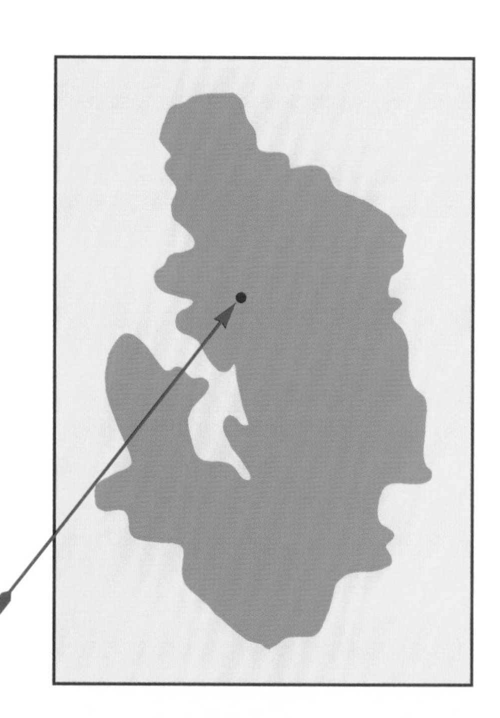

Illustration Copyright